why an author writes to a guy holding a fish

LAILA HALABY

why an author writes to a guy holding a fish

POEMS

FLORIDA | NEW YORK

www.2leafpress.org

2LEAF ❦ PRESS

P.O. Box 4378
Grand Central Station
New York, New York 10163-4378
editor@2leafpress.org
www.2leafpress.org

2LEAF PRESS INC. is a Florida-based
nonprofit 501(c)(3) organization that promotes
multicultural literature and literacy.
www.2leafpressinc.org

Cover art: © Laila Shawa

Book design and layout: Gabrielle David

Library of Congress Control Number: 2021915314

ISBN-13: 978-1-7374465-3-8 (Paperback)
ISBN-13: 978-1-7374465-5-2 (eBook)

10   9   8   7   6   5   4   3   2   1

Published in the United States of America

2Leaf Press trade distribution is handled by University of Chicago Press / Chicago Distribution Center (www.press.uchicago.edu) 773.702.7010. Titles are also available for corporate, premium, and special sales. Please direct inquiries to the UCP Sales Department, 773.702.7248.

POEMS

ACKNOWLEDGMENTS

THANK YOU TO ZOETIC PRESS and Riggerwelter Press for publishing different versions of some of the poems in this collection.

I am grateful to Gabrielle David for adding me to 2Leaf Press' roster, to Gail Hochman for looking out for me and my work, and to Helene Atwan for championing me. Laila Shawa, I am still giddy that your art covers my poems.

More than a decade has passed since the writing of most of these poems, and some of the people who encouraged and loved me then are no longer in my life. Here, I acknowledge them as they were.

To my incredible village of lovelies: Alice Dark, Ami Dalal, Andrew Barber, Anne Bullock, Anoushka Sharifi, Behnoush Sharifi, Careema Sleiman, Carmon Singleton, Clarence Harper, Emily Clark, Evelyn Villegas, Houri Berberian, Howe Gelb, Jon Vaffis, Kaiser Kuo, Khaled Sleiman, Margaret Halaby, Marianna Pegno, Marwan Mahmoud, Noreen Carver, Raad Zaghloul, Rabiah Zaghloul, Rebecka Macias, Reem Anouti, Rhody Downey, Robin Brande, Robin Zenger, Rula Khalidi, Santiago

Tso, Thabet Khalidi, Theresa Paquette, Tupac Shakur, and Waltraud Nichols.

If I left out your name, please forgive me.

Rebecka and Theresa, you facilitated the resurfacing of these stories and helped to bring me back from a very sad place. For that, I will always be grateful.

Houri, Rhody, Traudi, Santiago, Rula, Noreen, Annie, Evelyn, and Andy, you received my broken stories and tears with such kindness and love. And patience.

Evelyn, you made time to debrief and translate. Remember all those times you said, "You have to write a book about this stuff!"? Well, guess what?

Annie, you were there to pick up the pieces. Rula, you kept watch. Noreen, you found the bright side. (And read so many of my writings.) Carmon, you encouraged my power. Houri, you stood by me in tears and in laughter. (A lot of laughter.) (And you read so many of my writings.)

Mom, I am grateful to have your always-support and belief in me and in my writing, as well as (I never thought I'd say this) your critical eye. The combo has helped me to be better. In all things.

Raad and Rabiah, my beautiful boys, you are the guiding light in my days, the joy in my moments, and you continue to remind me what matters.

—Laila Halaby
December 2021

PROLOGUE:

~~wife.~~ woman.

boots

kick-ass
rugged
soft brown leather
last forever

we are
getting used to one another
my boots
and I

walking
on asphalt
fast
places await

men drive by
looking
I unpeel their eye
watch

from my body
kick it
in the air
land it in the dirt

no harm
looking
a cheater told me
you're beautiful

powerful
is what I am

you look at all women
the same

no. you're different
said the liar
I am
but not in the way you think

these boots
walk me straight
while I read
don't trip me up

boots
boots boots
a friend repeated
don't

Houri
told her
it sounds ugly
boots in *Armenian*

means cunt

these boots
and me walking
right now
we are mighty

kick
all that ugliness
to the side

step
        forward

twisted acacia

crumbly black bark
coated twisty limbs
the gigantic bonsai
stood crooked guard
in front of our house

long before we moved in
the tree had fallen
was righted
wrong
three feet of its trunk
parallel to the ground

our boys played games
around the tree
dodged its lethal prickers
when they buried dead pets
between its roots
or hung Halloween ghosts
from its creepy boughs

nubs
riddled the branches
from years of
boring beetles
treat it soon
or the whole tree will weaken
a neighbor told me

I kept an eye on the nubs
but never treated that condition

the night
before my husband moved out for good
he took some things
to his new apartment
while a fierce storm hurtled itself
through our neighborhood

violent winds
threw trash cans for blocks
ripped bushes out of the ground
knocked trees into houses

my older son looked out the window
sobbed at the sight of our crazy tree
lying stretched across the front path
as though it had gotten tired
of waiting for his father

the next day
I called in experts

it can be righted
said one

I'm not sure it will make it
said another

take it out and start fresh
said my oldest friend

one bright morning
four matching men
unloaded shiny shears and rakes

trimmed
the prickly canopy
lightening its heavy load

I explained the angle
the crookedness
the perfect imbalance of the tree
to the leader of the tidy men
he nodded
then tied a rope
from his truck
around the tired trunk
and pulled

even with all that trimming
the tree was so heavy
it tipped the truck

I took my children
to school
came back

alone

our hobbled tree
stood
trimmed and tall
its trunk vertical
as though it had been
folded in prayer all those years
and had finally gotten up to finish

sorry, ma'am
the roots snapped when we pulled it up
it may not make it

the leader of the tidy men told me
as he handed me a bill
for $395

why did you force it upright?
I shouted

he stared blankly
at my rage
there are no guarantees

maybe they couldn't believe
a tree growing at such an odd angle
could have existed
or thought it would look better
standing the way most trees do

maybe they just didn't listen

in three days
the twisted acacia
lost all its leaves
stood naked
staked
dead
in front of our house
as it remained
for months

until
a man driving down the street
looking for work
offered to take the whole thing down
for sixty dollars

in less than an hour

amputated dead branches
lay neatly piled
in a heap
by the side of our front path

my younger son stood beside me
as we watched the man load his truck
mama, do you remember that night?
the tree didn't want him to leave
it couldn't go on without him

anniversary

tomorrow marks seventeen years
that you took a sick day
to drive downtown
and marry me

I wore all the somethings
> old
> new
> borrowed
> blue

along with my pressed arrogance
that believed our perfect union
could be legalized on a sick day
without repercussions

no
shaykh was present
no
henna designs soaked my hands and feet

I should have known
should have demanded
expensive
and unwanted
formal rituals

I sit today
less poor
with the same longing:
to spin
beautiful
in the open palm
of a man who loves me

BOOK ONE:

woman. ~~wife.~~

adjectives

I spent nineteen years
with a man
who never told me I was beautiful
leading me to the conclusion
that I was not

shatra
habibti
helwa
in our early years
but not
beautiful

after we split
I was assailed by vocabulary
I did not recognize
hot
sexy
beautiful
words I had not thought applied to me

disorienting
to be spoken to
in a different language
takes a while to
understand the nuances

they say
women make bad choices
when they go on vacation
wooed by exotic

tongues
that spin words
all kinds of pretty

easy to lose your
self
inside a trip abroad

listen

our family is shattered
into sharp edges and hollow spaces
like the back window
blown open by the Jerusalem paper weight

the days march on
oblivious to my heartbreak

at work
I bury my story
in other people's business

listen

to this patient who
had been with a gentleman
who had AIDS
didn't tell her
until he passed it onto her
and then died of it

alone and ostracized from her world
she grabbed the reins of her life
learned to live again
quit fearing
sings in her church choir
love and God are everywhere
rates everything a perfect ten

listen

to this patient
an Iraqi artist

who lived through war
is now soaked in the loneliness of exile
his only solace in painting
you have to trust love in all its forms!
and enjoy life!
and eat cheeseburgers!
we laugh like old friends

listen

the first coffee date I
have after my divorce

lock and load
he says
you never know
he says
about Iraqis crossing checkpoints
his hands coming together
around an imaginary machine gun

you just never know
when people
(who looked like my father
my brothers
my ex-husband
my sons
me)
come close

his eyes are flat
one tooth is chipped
his nails are jagged
the skin on his surprisingly small hands is dry
hair shaved close
military style
with an extra flap up top

I want to fix and trim and moisturize

we are seeing if we like each other
(we don't particularly)

(though he tells a good story)
(and supposedly can sing too)

he has just said *fucker* for the twenty-third time

we don't meet again
because of the war

and also because

alliances

dangerous men

a generation ago
when my cousin lived in New York City
and had to take the subway at night
she'd go up to the biggest
scariest-looking man on the platform
tell him she was nervous to be there alone
and could she stand with him
he always agreed
and she always got home safely

Arab blood
should have promised me
a lifetime of safe alliances
but my lineage came tainted in shame
lost me rights
to property
security
got erased
by father
brother
husband

standing on the platform of this American ride
my safe way home surrounds me
with all matter of fierce
the biggest ex-con
user
marine
private
sergeant
boxer

construction worker
prison guard
border patrol
all tough and edges

I am not nervous

safe woman

falling

I admit

I fall in love
easily
about every six months
and yes
even during the last couple years
of my marriage

so maybe it wasn't love
I was falling into

I'd come across
a delightful person
twinkly eyes
a good story
and be smitten
fall into possibility

it happened everywhere
at the grocery store
waiting to pick up my boys

clean and quiet
words and glances
love was everywhere
except in my home

what if
all those years of wanting
unfulfillable longing
trying to do the right thing

translates

not
into love
but into a tsunami
of something else?

the dream it would have been better to forget

last night
I dreamed about my husband

not the one who left

this man
was the husband
I had yet to meet
     bald
     Italian
     in his forties
     lean
     not too tall
     he had creases on his face
     and light in his eyes

when I woke up
I felt hopeful

new love

land me gently
between the pages
of your life
not a bookmark
or pressed flower
no passing-through visitor
that could
get lost
but the ink itself
seeped into paper
permanent print
words
details

together
we are the story

the man from my dream

he smiles at me
    with creases around his eyes
sto cercando la mia socia

even as I suspect he Google-translated this
    the Italian
    bald head
    light in his eyes
feel like destiny

I respond
mi hai trovata

delighted
relieved
my tired heart
exits the freeway
parks under a eucalyptus tree

weeks
of interesting conversation
and restaurant dining
consume me

contrary to my nature
I never offer to pay
which nags at me
more than anything

until the dreams start

first dream

> a cheery motel in LA with my kids
> a knock at the door
> the day has turned cloudy
> the motel lot is deserted
> three men in Halloween masks
> stand with machine guns
> pointed at my children

I wake up
with a scream in my mouth

what does it mean? I ask Andy

you worry too much

second dream

> Heidi our beloved dachshund
> is being sliced up like lunch meat
> and offered to everyone at my work

I wake up
heart pounding

third dream

> his mother in a faded housedress
> holds my hand
> *be patient with him*
> *he's got to figure things out*
> *you are The One*

fourth dream

> arm in arm at the county fair
> in the middle of a dusty crowd
> he transforms from his handsome self
> into a serial killer death-row inmate horror movie old man
> I try to pull away
> but can't release myself from his iron grip
> we keep walking

I wake up screaming

fifth dream

> *you don't deserve him*
> his dead mother tells me
> *he is better than you*

sixth dream

> in front of my house
> he pops up outside my car
> all the muscles in his face pulled tight
> he is going to kill me

I wake up screaming

what does it mean?
I ask Andy

that you are eating something really weird before you sleep

Andy is a chemist
and since I like his version
better than mine

that he is not who he seems to be
(who I want him to be)
that I must protect my children
and in his presence I will not be able to do that
he is dangerous
and he lies

I've had more nightmares in two weeks
than in the preceding twenty years

I take each one
fold it into a tiny silken package
tuck it under my mattress

and wait

a kiss

is not a commitment
signed contract
life promised to someone

no one cares
if you date
who you date

no one's talking
behind your back
phoning your father

reporting on your activities
date, kiss, fuck
if you want to

honey
this is America
2009

you are free
to do
as you please

go to a man's house
love him
all night

but don't get confused
a kiss
don't mean

anything
anymore

writer/liar

I accuse you
of lexiconic irresponsibility
general assholery

being loosey goosey
with your words
piles of rose petal
promises
cover my feet

like shit

fetid and hideous

Margie and Tupac and me on my last date with the supposed-to-be-forever guy

or

it took ghosts talking for me to see clearly

for Rula, Thabet, and Reem, who reminded me what love should feel like

my body
began rejecting him
the first time he went away
tensed
at the something-wrong-with-this-picture

even as every pore screamed at me to let go
my heart was stubborn
clung to its first knowing
        bald
        Italian
        in his forties
        lean
        not too tall

I ignored the aches
and nightmares
my body released
in protest
to my heart's blindness

during his second trip away
my brain pleaded

with my impatient self
to accept his words at face value
keep busy, do some home improvement
my wise self advised

with each beat of my hammer
squeeze of the caulk tube
swipe of the paint brush
he slipped further away
got closer to a could-have-been

only my stupid heart held on

mighty
after Margie's memorial service
her spirit accompanies me while I get ready
for my last date
with the supposed-to-be-forever guy

I blast Tupac
line my eyes black with kohl
dance with lightness around the house
feel the relief from here

more uptight than usual
he steps into my sweet home
muscle and pretensions
slamming into Tupac's smooth

love you, Mama
my boys tell me
when I call them at their father's
to wish them sweet sleeps

the glory and power of my sons
yanks the last tendril of fantasy
out of my heart
pins my eyes open

> this poseur
> over-thinker
> master-controller
> been flicking me
> onto his guarded barbed fence
> while he woman-searches
> lifts me off
> when he wants company
> or a good laugh

he has chosen
a well-reviewed South American restaurant
where we sit across from each other
amid soft lighting and the gentle buzz of talking

I study his
> bald head
> handsome face
> knit brow
as he studies the wine list

what kind do you like? he asks
red I reply
he pauses and his eyes narrow
fruity? not too much tannin?

did he for real just ask you that?
Tupac asks from across the table
his dark eyes are smiling huge
girl, you are wasting your time with this clown

Tupac comes around and scoots in next to me
when the waitress leans
close close over the shoulder
of the supposed-to-be-forever guy

she points to items on his menu
he looks up at her with questions
it occurs to me they would make a nice couple
though I suspect he would never date a waitress

bring us a taste of the A Lisa Malbec he tells her

I study the menu
fantasizing about the plantains I am about to order
when he smiles wide
they are famous for their plantation dishes

Margie's body shakes with giggles
Tupac stands up
half indignant
half laughing
holds out his hand
demanding we leave this made-for-TV scene

when I don't budge
he sits back down and grins
you know what? eat your hundred-dollar plantation meal

all confidence and charm
I indulge the-supposed-to-be-forever-guy's flips
of the conversation
so we're still talking about him
act like I am in control
which I suppose I am
for the first time in this this

which isn't going to be a this
in a couple of hours

after our Malbec
plantains
and superficial meaningful conversation
we get up to leave
walk tall through a gauntlet of watching

we drive home
my two angels in the back seat
Margie belting out *hold on*
Tupac saying I should keep my eyes on the prize
and he's not it

now
we're in front of my house
sitting in his $50,000 car

you don't make me feel amazing
I tell him

he slumps forward for the camera
so now I don't make you feel amazing?

it is all about him, says Tupac

the-supposed-to-be-forever-guy rubs his eyes
White man crocodile tears
whispers a ghost from the back seat

I step into the night
reach my arms up
let the stars kiss my face

Margie and Tupac
watch me from the corner
hug each other tight under the brilliant sky
and go their separate ways

I step back
into my life

BOOK TWO:

other. woman.

my bed

is heaven

in the dark quiet
of the day's waking
my rested body stretched out
diagonal and still sleepy
stories at my fingertips

in the evening
squirming children
gleeful in my cuddles
or in the dog's disobedience
that has her resting on my pillows

you really want to give that up?

private

shake off
thoughts
of difference
in age
background
life goals

blink away
pictures
of camouflage
m-16's
IED's

new world order
looks at details
not the big picture

give me your mouth
to put over mine
when our lips touch
they move
with the same rhythm

with your tongue
alongside mine
we taste
in the same language

you've only been
gone a few hours

but I wander the house searching for traces
a hair or two
one of your black t-shirts
a note
even a fingerprint
would do

I find nothing

I give up
strip down to shower

pausing in front of the mirror
looking for changes
smoother skin
or shinier hair
but I see nothing different

about to turn away
wash off the last hint of you
my eyes rest on something
improbable
impossible
and utterly gorgeous

on my right side
spanning from hip to breast
is the clear indentation
of your hand
that held me

caressed me
brought me out of an anguished stupor

I place my hand over yours
close my eyes
and squeeze
until the longing recedes
just a bit

the peace process

acoustic
relentless
authentic
heaven

words pass
through my mind
when my mind
can poke itself out
of the ocean depths
of delight
my body
has dropped into

you
so unlikely
hard to my soft
white to my brown
generous to my selfish
fill me again
and again
I can't get enough

soldier-symbol
occupier
invader
colonial oppressor

in your presence
I am the sun
stars
a beauty queen

don't bring me flowers
or gifts in crinkly paper boxes
held tight
by waxy ribbons

don't waste my time
in places
called *elle*
or *ciao*

put your tongue
in my mouth
kiss me
all night

and don't ever lie

who wanted who first?
my kaffiyeh
your ACU

tangled up

thinking of you

I saw two butterflies
small and orange
the light bounced off the incandescent spots
on their wings

they flitted about
one paralleling the other's
flaps and drops
then reversing

they did this
in the middle of the street
at my eye level
joyful for a few blinks

flirty moments
of orange and bright
that felt like love
and was over in minutes

suspicion

is back

nagging doubt
sureness
that you've left out
a crucial part
of this story
the wife-part
the detail
that will have me
sobbing sometime soon

I am stronger than this
take it for what it is
enjoy the beauty
of the moment

spectacle

that man
I spent some months with
came to my house

early one morning
to confess
that he was engaged

that his *girl*
of four years
had found out about me

I had a glorious
righteous moment
slapped him upside the head

in front of my sweet house
on my quiet street
as dog-walking, eyebrow-raised neighbors walked past

no regrets
no wish-I-hads
no-if-onlys

I emptied every ugly thought from my mind
drenched him in my words
watched fire drops splash onto the cold asphalt

and sizzle

he hung his head
a giant boy with no conscience

if I had daughters
I would tell them
don't be suckers for empty words

trust your gut
love yourself
honor the beauty that is you

but I have sons
so I tell them
don't ever lie

to bend a woman's wishes your way
or you answer to me
and I will slap you upside the head

for everyone to see

I am the white devil

you said

what does that make me?
I asked

twice

you had no answer
not even a funny one

give up?
you didn't care enough to think about it

a brown angel
(heaven with an attitude)

you lied to me
seven times
(at least)
one for each of God's days

on the seventh lie
God couldn't take it any more

enough messing with my employees
I imagine Him saying
(God has an attitude too)

the next day
that fiancée of yours
(the one I didn't know you had)

figured out that you are
what I long suspected you to be

I don't know the outcome
(my powers have their limitations)
but I do know this:

only a fool keeps lying
with an angel standing in front of him

colonizer

white man
soaked in selfish
bring out the cruel in me
drag my occupied voice
and many-hundred-year-old
righteous soul
to the surface
shine light on
the love inked under my skin
by generations
of disenfranchised sistas

white man
come into my life
spin all kind of words pretty
like they real
not copped off a TV show
not the next poem he gonna write
use words like
first
unique
beautiful
translation:
exotic
freaky
other

white man
blow me off
after he take his notes
ain't got time
for nothing
but the writing

expose us all naked
legs spread
show off his gift
purport like he a different kind of

white man
while he painting us
with our own sweat and bones
talk like he know
and those words
is all his
we just in his moment

look at that fool up there
taking his time
charming his audience
while he spread a paté
of brown woman blood and tears
on a hard white cracker
and lick his lips
wet
after
each
bite

liars

when I was younger
still innocent
I was shocked
when a co-worker my age
told me about an older neighbor
who had hit on her
as though he were a single man
not a father to three
husband to one

what wife?
asked that man who has been flirting with me for years
I raised my eyebrows
he laughed
like it was a joke that he was trying to erase the wife
he's already told me about
the life he's been living for the last generation

that same man came to my door the day after he found me
crying
to make sure you are okay
he said
who lied to you?
I imagined
for about five seconds
that he was going to find the jerk
and kick his ass

he hugged me
kissed me on the cheek
told me he was there for me
if you need anything

where's your car?
I asked
I parked it at the end of the street
so your neighbors wouldn't wonder

if I had let that man into my house
he would have tried to do the same damn thing
as the lying cheat
who made me cry

other

lifetime
spent
checking that damn box
other race
other ethnicity
product of
the other
woman

fought
to be whole
complete
no marginal
shamefulness

only to become one

a lifetime
of resistance
leads to this?

other woman
will not do

beads in my bed

it's been a week

I pull back
the newly laundered sheets
find three tiny clear beads
that must have migrated
from a child's pocket
pure and clean
each one

completely unlike
those bulky trade bead lies
you shoved carelessly
onto the fraying thread of your desire
until the whole thing broke
spatter-clattered across the floor
in a crazy dangerous mess
that still has people falling
all over themselves

strung together
I thought those beads were gorgeous
shattered between my fingers
each was nothing more
than painted glass
a hard tiny promise
with no currency

I remove the three mysterious visitors
put them on the bedside table
and slide between the clean cotton sheets
allow the heavy down to warm me

embrace me

my sweet bed
is rid of you

BOOK THREE:

modern woman.

why an author writes to
a guy holding a fish

online dating
in America
in your forties
after a lifetime
of Middle Eastern sensibility
and almost 20 years of marriage
requires resolve
patience
and some cross-cultural
understanding

first the emails:
the gross
do you know how to do that sexy Arabic dancing?
the self-absorbed
what might you like to learn next about me, young lady?
the philosophical
the trick in life is finding pleasure in the seemingly benign and
mundane
the decent
you seem like someone I'd like to know better

then the phone calls
where you get to learn
about his tasteful gated community
scuba diving experiences
six-figure job
or his attempts to find balance between his life's vision and
the choices he's made

first interview
over coffee or a drink
can be disconcerting
I need my 'me' time; sometimes I go antiquing or take baths
pleasant
*hard to make your life as an old-school journalist in this digital
day of blogs*
or terrific
*I haven't enjoyed having coffee with someone this much in I
don't know how long*

don't get lost yet
a fantastic conversation
means nothing
other than a second chance
even if he claims to be looking for forever
states that he wants a woman who is charming and intelligent
(like him)
hints that you possess the proper qualifications

mealtime dating
can hang around for weeks
like a nosy neighbor
while he's comparison shopping
checking into your credentials
(these *are* a series of interviews
to find the best candidate for the post
in his exclusive company)

even though there's texting
(flirtatious, sexy)
and kisses on the cheek or mouth
intimate brushings of hands on bodies
you do not have the job yet
and chances are
he's holding several other interviews

this is where I slam into the walls of my raising
trip over rules
and grandma voices
telling me decent girls
don't

let a man put his hands all over you if he don't mean it
(sex is not an agility test)
wait around while a man decides if he wants you enough
(if he hasn't figured it out by now, he's not the one)
put up with a man who doesn't have time to call
(he got woman prints still on him)
strings you along because it makes *him* feel good

I've changed my mind
I am no longer interested in this position
it does not meet my needs
or make me feel amazing
and all this drawn-out small talk
in pricey restaurants
is getting on my ever-last nerve

I want a real man who does what he says he's going to do
kisses me like he means it
and don't spread it around
like he's all that

a guy holding a fish

all man
in his walk
talk
looks
and tender touches
sweet lips brushing your neck
gentle mightiness
pushing you up
against a wall
to kiss you
just right
grab your ass
power
mixed in
with serious affection

doesn't matter
your days are different
your hearts unlock
with the same key

let him love you

transmission

two days after
a patient told me
that his adult daughter
got so sick with the flu
she had to be hospitalized
and one day after Steve emailed
saying he could barely get out of bed
going on two weeks now
which is why he hasn't called
and hopefully no one sweeps you off your feet
before I get better
I stand in line at the pharmacy
to get the flu shot I've postponed
for two months because I'm a little nervous
having never had one before

two Saturdays ago
if Steve had called
like he said he was going to
and we had gone out
like I had half-heartedly agreed to
and I had kissed him goodnight
as I might have if things had gone well
I could be the one hospitalized

but Steve didn't call
instead C wrote a sweet note
that drove home and parked in the garage my desire
not for a man with slick qualifications
but for someone down-to-earth who makes me feel good
am lost in line at the pharmacy
with thoughts of how happy C makes me feel
when I notice a crumpled older man staring at me

you look just like my daughter
he says, panic falling out of his mouth
she does her hair the same way
she's the same height as you
and she lives in New Rochelle, New York
for some reason I expected him to say
Scotland or Canada
you kinda scared me
his gray face holds too much sadness
and I hope his seeing me
will get him to call his daughter
maybe remind her to get a flu shot
so he doesn't have to worry about
someone else taking her to the hospital
if she gets sick

ma'am, says the pharmacist
who looks young enough to be my daughter
though much too blond and arrogant
what was your question?
she looks irritated as I explain
that I had been allergic to eggs as a child
and should I check off the box
stating this allergy
I will not give you a flu shot today
she tells me, bursting with her own power
you will have to go to your doctor's office
I resist the urge to tell her off
and sweetly inform her that I was fifteen
the last time I had a reaction
to eggs and even then it was only hives
I will not give you a shot today
her face is rigid and confident
as she goes over to help the gray man
whose daughter I remind him of
leaving me to walk away and call my doctor

I was allergic to eggs when I was a kid
and I always get the flu shot
the girl who answers the phone tells me
and after she quizzes me about my reaction to eggs
disagrees with the dictator pharmacist
suggests I go to a different drug store
which I plan to do this weekend
but get distracted by soccer games
and C's invitation to come over for pizza
and meet his children
which I do though I barely know him
give Rula his address and phone number
just in case
don't hear her call or see her text messages
until I'm driving home at eleven
full with his taste in my mouth
hoping he doesn't have the flu

disclosure

aside from the one
who clawed at my windows
for more than a decade
because he couldn't find
the emergency exit
no man has ever been
brave enough
to hold me
for more than the time
it took him
to get off

too much
words
falling all over the place
slick with expecting
trip them up
too much
dreams
gigantic in their stretch
knock every last one
down the staircase
thump thump
crash
in a million loud pieces
that bloody my feet for years
too much
moving
slams into their desire
to watch
I can sit still
when I die

like a teenage boy
at an all-you-can-eat buffet
greedy with the possibility
of having it all
I can't never fill
my forever-lasting empty

close down
to the option of love
write my stories
raise my boys
until I catch a glint
a glimmering maybe
grab on too hard
skewer my hand
watch another man
flee the tsunami
of my too much
bleeding out
proof I am
that broken bastard
my bones know me to be

but in that crooked
bastard self
is magic
the kind that wins countries
stitches up wounds
loves you
passionate
fierce
happy
and forever

you gonna let me drench you
in the crazy river

of my too much
loving?
from this side
seems like
you man enough
to keep your own
solid self
upright
dry
in tact

fill me
again
and again
and again

don't wanna be

your forgotten
don't-have-time-right-now
when-I-get-a-chance-I'll-read-it
girl
front stoop
waiting for a sweep
holey socks
old stink
crusted-up plates
piled in the sink
dusty floor
don't even wanna be
your good shirt
folded in a drawer
waiting on a conversation

don't wanna be
tit for tat
this for that
sliver of soap
too small to use
the wish-I-had
in your memory
the what-was-her-name
in your mouth

wanna be
your basketball
coffee bean
comfy bed
all-star team
favorite word
ice cream

time we don't have
poem on a page
icing finger-licked
off your cake
that best part
sits on your tongue
makes you grin

wanna be
the quiet
in your morning
the laugh
in your voice
the moist
to your dry
the towel
to your sweat
the hard
between your legs

wanna be
your all-that
girl

friday morning

it's been a couple of hours
since you left my warm bed
Friday morning
is happening on my street

men who look like you
are renovating the white brick house
a few doors down
where an older white man lived
with his dying white wife
I only ever saw twice

their windows spent most of the time
covered by heavy curtains
and no one ever visited
neither of them looked happy
a lifetime of together
hammered apart by illness
or infidelity
or general incompatibility

I'd see him walking home
with a young Asian woman
who'd always say goodbye
a couple of blocks away
or sometimes drop him off
at the corner

they never kissed
but they did hold hands
and while at least thirty years separated them
it was clear they had both found

some kind of peace
in the other

I never saw the family leave
don't know if the dying wife
finally died
or if they just decided to sell
will never know if that older man
stayed with the young woman
who held his hand
pulled him away

it is still Friday morning outside
those men are removing the last unfaithful traces
from the white brick house a few doors down
while I lie safe and content in my sweet bed
with the shadow of all 75 inches of you still holding me
at peace for the first time in years
full with the joy of accepting
another human being into my life
flaws and all

closest thing to perfect

for C

you said you'd come over
for a little while
and not to go to any trouble

I sliced the leftover steak
into tiny pieces
diced onions and fried them together
chopped lettuce
grated cheese
mixed the guacamole
opened bags of chips and tortillas
heated beans
rinsed strawberries
set the table
vacuumed the living room
and wiped down the bathroom

you arrived
freshly showered
shaved and pressed
my heart filled
with your presence
your decision
to have dinner
with me and my younger son

the two of you talked radio stations
music, sports, and school
while you built your tacos
ate your chips
both of you content and relaxed

I told a story
a truck driver patient
had told me
about a woman
who had thrown herself
under the wheels of his friend's truck
as he was exiting the freeway

was she crazy? you asked
I started to tell her story
how her husband had died
in that same spot
like I said, crazy
you put your food down
there is nothing bad enough
can happen to you
that it is not worth getting up
the next day to see the sun

the firmness of your belief
filled your eyes
and not for the first time
in the few short months
I've known you
I felt love for the man you are

after dinner
my son found his best friend
brought him over
to play basketball
the kids outside
you stood behind me
pulled me close to your body
wrapping me up in your arms
filling me with wanting
the way you always do

in the cool evening
doors open
we cleared the table
emptied mouse traps
snuck kisses
the boys challenged you
to a two-on-one
and beat you
under clouds of dust

you had to leave early
to prepare your house
for your children's arrival
and when you kissed me goodbye
it felt so utterly real and right
that I had to catch my breath

later you told me
that dinner was very good
and eating with me and my son
was as close to a perfect moment
as you could have asked for

whatever happens
in the months to come
I will cherish
this storybook evening
be grateful
for the love that filled my house

the space between us

does not involve time zones
thousands of miles
or checkpoints
no gang territory
clan affiliation
hostile soldiers
drought or floods
separate us

just a few streets
a mall
two jobs
two houses
four children
my motherhood
and your unfulfilled dreams

Tupac

countless times
you've rocked me
soft and sweet
as I lay sobbing on my couch

you'd promise that everything
was gonna be all right
and I had to keep my head up

guardian angel
when it comes to men
why you own the voice in my head
escapes me

be strong
you'd say
reminding me that the man I was busy crying over
was just a man
can't have the good without the bad

I feel like I should assert my feminist rights
over something here
like the fact that I am dating a liar
maybe a player
or that it's your voice in my head

you
velvet-eyed
sugar-love
guardian angel
my UN-appointed interpreter
here to translate player-man for me
whenever my mighty self

gets complacent
and I start acting a fool
like now
doubled over in the middle of the street
breath stolen by sobs
because I know that man is cheating

girl, you gotta keep your head up

B678206

dawn highway driving
two unplanned weeks stretch in front of me
like a childhood afternoon:
happy and full of possibility

twenty miles out of town
a white Louisiana pick-up truck parallels our speed
pulling in front
or dropping just behind

the middle-aged driver
spends his time smoking
talking on his phone
drinking milk, singing
and smiling when he passes us

both my boys doze
in the early morning light
while my thoughts battle
between what I know
and what I want to believe

miles unfold beneath us
sweet in the relax of driving
content in the company
of the animated Mr. Louisiana

we'll lose him for good
at Eloy
Casa Grande
Florence
surely Phoenix

when we clear
that sixth largest city
in the nation
at the same speed
it feels like friends

dropping back to let the other in
waving as we pass
winking and relaxed
pleasant and considerate company
on our early morning desert drive

after 243 miles of traveling together
we exit at Quartzite
turning opposite directions
in search of gas
wave goodbye

you texted during that ride
asking me if I was on my way
to paradise

I do not answer

the bee

today I went running
seven hundred and sixty miles away
from you and your sudden need to go slow

after months spent with you
your children
your friends
you started lying about all kinds of things
including taking a job in another state

these thoughts
ricocheted around my tired head
as I raced myself
up the slope of the road
taking in giant breaths

a tiny bee
flew in my mouth

I stopped
leaned over
to spit it out
but only half of it came up
my throat stinging
I had somehow gulped down

half a bee

twenty years ago
I was stung
by more than twenty bees
you could have a really bad reaction if you are ever stung again
Anoushka's nurse mother told me

nothing left to spit
I continued my run up Tassajara
waiting on the predicted *bad reaction*
that would drop me dead
by the side of the road
in a city that is not mine
on a vacation
that is meant to be rejuvenating
and happy

instead of thinking about you
I checked in on my life

      I am the woman I want to be
          don't need to be your girlfriend
          to feel my power

      I am the mother I need to be
          don't need a man
          to raise my boys

funny how it takes half a bee
hurtling through a body
to recognize the wings
I've had all this time

yes, there were dreams with this one too

first dream (a week after we met)

> we walk up the stairs of a theater
> arm in arm
> he holds a folder of my writing
> my wallet
> and my broken phone
>
> he places my things on the floor
> at a landing halfway up
> kisses me
> and watches
> as I ascend the remaining stairs

what does it mean?
I asked Andy

that he will keep you company
even when you go places he's not interested in going

since I liked his version
better than mine

> he respects your writing
> your ability to take care of yourself
> but he will disregard your personal life
> and only be able to accompany you
> up to a certain point

I fold this flimsy handkerchief of a dream
tuck it under a mattress at the back of my mind

months of accompanying him
while he played darts
a trip to the lake
while he fished and I wrote

not idyllic but nice
until he was on trial for drunk driving
from before I met him
spent a night in jail

the next week I was called for jury duty
on a DUI case
has anyone you know
been convicted of a DUI?

I raised my hand
and when I was called back
the judge and attorneys asked *who?*

I struggled with the right word
ended up with *boyfriend*
though it felt jagged in my mouth

I was dismissed from the jury pool

at dinner a few nights later
I told him what they had asked me
and you said it was a friend

I unfolded the handkerchief

second dream (summer)

> I am driving down a steep street
> through a house
> where I see him standing in the kitchen
> kissing a woman

I don't need to ask Andy
what this one means

how I got my life back

are you that fucking naïve?
you once asked me
when I told you about the man
whose been flirting with me for years
he only wants to sleep with you

like a slap in the face
an eyeball into your brain
I've known him eleven years
we talk about everything
we're friends

your fury, I see now
stems from your own desires
your inability to look at a woman
without thinking about sex

my angel band steps in for debriefing

Andy: *this was a power thing*
he has it all; he never invested
in you the person; for him women
are life-support systems for vaginas

Evelyn: *you needed to experience this*
so you know what you don't want
now you can be choosey

Santiago: *go get your life back*
get your you, the happy one
and no man worth crying over
is ever gonna make you cry

Annie: *take a break and live your life*
enjoy your children and your writing
don't even think about guys for awhile

Carmon: *write a letter to God*
ask for the exact man you want
then put the letter away
and live your life

my man-request letter to God/the universe/myself

he gotta have goodness
with an edge
but not a destructive one
an understanding way
honesty
deep
his own self
gotta be enough intact
that he can truly love
(tall and hot and athletic and my age would be nice)
(along with the ability to build and fix stuff)
bravery
to stand up for what he believes in
and to love me
and the dude gotta be funny
not frivolous
someone who brings out my good
who's patient
not self-absorbed
or selfish
and who never makes me feel insecure
he gotta have
joyousness
acceptance
integrity
emotional stability
wisdom
not a diva
let him be smart
not pompous
open to the arts

but not necessarily in them
someone I can lean on
who will truly appreciate me
for me
and let him be faithful
and an amazing lover

amen

for a minute I let myself believe
my prayers were answered

this true thing
not caught up in hectic
or zooming away
contrails at its heels
no snags
no leftover unhappy
dripping ugly
between the cracks

this is sunshine
beach sitting
naked clean
fast riding
fat clouds
gentle fingers
holding
probing
deep
power
this is

magic
the earthly kind
soft grass between toes
fresh tomatoes
rock and roll
juicy burgers
peanuts and beer
perfect balance
fingers locked
lips soft

skin wet
giant laughter
and gentle
hope
for good

with you
I am me
no folding
to fit
a different mold
baby with you
I feel complete
home safe
warm
cherished

and you seem
so damn sure

slaying the ghul

first dream (two weeks after we met)

> sitting in the big red chair
> *pop pop*
> someone stands over me
> fires a gun
> twice
> into the base of my neck

what does it mean?
I asked Andy

that you are watching too many cop shows before bed

since I preferred his answer to mine

> two pops at your neck
> and you are still alive
> means be careful
> he will forsake your children
> if it serves his needs

I folded this silk handkerchief of a dream
tucked it under a mattress at the back of my mind

second dream (months later)

> the phone rings
> his ex-wife
> asks about my son's dentist appointment
> calls back three more times
> as if she has some business in my life

I woke up next to him
demanding an explanation
my ex-wife is a rock
we have been apart
for almost a year
I have no feelings for her
I don't even like her
I think I loved her
but that's been over
for a really long time

even as he talked
I knew
that she was taking up too much space

months have passed
since his constant talk
of living together
buying a house
that would accommodate us all
traveling the world
sharing his million-dollar portfolio
his house is sold
his next steps unclear

I cringed at his plans
to stay with his ex-wife
for free
I need to get out of the heat
spend time in the northwest
but I want you in my life
I will come back in August

we filled the back of a moving truck
with his few belongings
while the day crept up into triple digits
after his giant house
was emptied and cleaned
my boys carried his things
from truck to storage locker

late afternoon
he suggested
to the kids' delight
that we eat out

we were in my home
where he would be staying
for a few days
before his departure
it was seven
everyone showered and hungry
I've spent enough money today
let's make burgers instead
I stared at him
if it were just us I wouldn't mind
he said when the boys were out of earshot

too tired and hungry to argue
we drove in silence while I unfolded
that tiny forgotten handkerchief
shook it out across my lap
carried it with me inside the grocery store
felt it double
triple
quadruple in size
wrap around me
when he handed me ten dollars
my contribution

I threw it back at him loudly
I don't want your money
do not need your money

felt it smothering me
along with the averted glances
of the cashier
and customers behind us

endings

empty promises
couldn't sustain me
as I extricated him from my life
broke up
deleted
unfriended
unfollowed
I came across a post
he wrote on his ex-wife's wall
a few weeks after we met

I LOVE you!!!!

last dream

      parked
at the top of a steep hill
I have to back my truck out
and navigate the curvy pitched road
the entire way dotted with tiny children
I drive turtle slow
windows down

I pat heads of toddlers
as I go

when I reach the bottom
where he waits for me
the children face me and applaud

he signals that I should park
but I turn left
and continue driving

appropriation

you put your arms
through the sleeves
of my motherhood
thought you could fit
enjoyed looking at your hands
wiggling and free

but when you started to feel
the tight squeeze
of responsibility
you began peeling it off
slowly
layer by layer

see that pile in the corner
so colorful
heaps of yarn
heaps of my life

and not a single trace of you

con man

I took up
with a hollow man
empty soul
disguised as
my perfect

I let him in
to my home
and family
impressed by his ability
to travel light
and adapt

was asleep
when he dragged in stacks
of empty trunks
suitcases, boxes, and mason jars
tried to fill them
with every single thing
that mattered to me

it happened sneaky
quiet
and slow

at first

then I caught him
wrapping my words in newspaper
and sending them to another woman
erasing steps in my age-old recipes
then trying to convince me
I had them wrong

he lied
to cover his empty
backed out of promises
he mocked me
baited my ex-husband

he denied every broken window
with a baseball mitt on his hand
and a flood of crocodile tears

it took me some months
to slice him out
of my heart
though really
he was just barely in the door
propped open
with his jars and boxes of empty

I woke up one morning
gave him a giant shove
and changed the locks
on my house
my heart
my life

that empty man
is gone

the gardeners

when you are born in the wrong place

or

when you are born in the right place
but taken away

you seek familiar skies
stretching that can grow you a weird and crooked
the gardeners can't figure out

they'll sniff around your trunk
proclaim you exotic and fascinating
then get to work with their shears

meanwhile

your parts chase unlikely directions

the gardeners trim
add fertilizer
            (the toxins turn your leaves funny colors)

the gardeners post pictures on social media
and horticulture message boards
anybody have an idea how to make this lopsided thing grow right?

everyone has an idea

it'll stand straighter if you chop off those crooked limbs

I'm not sure it will make it if you do that

take it out and start fresh

the gardeners will try everything
nothing will work
they will throw their hands in the air

and go home to water their apple trees

BOOK FOUR:

woman. writer.

divorced in America with a name that carries eternal and unrequited love

cop
soldier
builder

walked into my life
cloaked in forever stories
the only uniform I recognized

I misread every sign
confused
guns
cargo pants
house repairs
beer
recreation
with imagined incompatible tribes

birthed in longing
schooled in never-extinguishing-the-lantern
them not measuring up
was tragedy that made sense
only in the aftermath

and then repeated

stalled on the frontage road
while just over the barricade
reality zoomed by
I watch ghost-like apparitions
rise above the flames

Qais
Romeo
Devdas

swirled together
in the blue of the sky
and then
gone

Andy and I were talking about our online dating experiences, and he asked me what I was looking for and I said, I was waiting on Odysseus, and he couldn't stop laughing

they deem themselves Prince Charmings
all sweet and words
pour sugar onto shit
and promise the world

intellectual
caught up in his own smarts
spins out hefty thinking
acts impressed/surprised I understand

soldier/cop/guard
hides his empty under a uniform
thinks my wild is refreshing
until he can't keep it down

broken men
come up from addictions/afflictions
wonder if I'm home plate
wonder if I can fill the job *woman wanted*

pot-bellied ex-classmates/random strangers
living in broken marriages
see my *beautiful and mysterious* face as the light
at the end of their boring domestic tunnel

old and young lined up in front of my cage
sticking their dicks through the bars
their pretty words seep
in a flood of stink

used to be I'd soak it all up
offer them tea and quiet
massage away their pains
while I considered the possibility

now I pace

in front of the maze I've built
with my stories and poems
my kids sheltered far enough inside
they don't hear the cat-calling

no one
is coming through these bars again
not even Odysseus
with his significant adventures

he waited too long
and I'm no Penelope
waiting waiting waiting
on possibility and hope

I took up with several of the suitors
Eurymachus was the smoothest and the worst
I kicked him out too
what kind of man is jealous of a woman's son?

no more waiting, stitching
the only time past childhood that I stitched

was when I had to lie down for months
so my sons wouldn't get born too soon

though no Anticlea
it's the sons I will wait for
Odysseus, this is my home
you are no longer welcome

pain

a few months after
the hollow man
was gone for good
I whirled around my house
in the dumb rush
of the morning

still
always
a little late
making lunch
finishing dishes
opening curtains

in a torn flash
of ugly
I wished unkind things
on that hollow man

unrepeatable
unkind things

I pulled back
the remaining curtain
from the window
that had once been hollowed
by the Jerusalem paper weight

the sun rushed into my back room
the one that was to be his office

in a final fit of fury
I slammed the door shut

leaving my thumb
stuck
in the whisper divide
between frame and door

I've given birth twice
once unmedicated
miscarried
had procedures
stitches
slashed my foot
on a rusty piece of metal
been the other woman

I thought I had learned
to hold my hurt quietly

but as this nickel-sized betrayal
pounded torment
throughout the rest of me
I howled
cursed
reeled around the room
for
many
many
many
minutes

the pain passed
as pain often does

months later
I sit in this same room
writing in the quiet
while the sun warms my face
my still disfigured thumb
its nail half grown back
rests on the black lacquered fountain pen
my once-husband
gave me
twenty years ago

the sun
fills my room

waking up

I stare
at my computer screen
my eyes a little crossed
not focused

I am aware
of my body
relaxed
content after a solid sleep
the tickle of my hair reaching down my back
stretched-out muscles in my legs
the desire to smile
my early morning writing
is neglected

again

not from exhaustion
anger
sadness

rather delight
at the feeling
of being here

starting life

all over again

alone/not alone surrounded by women in the art museum and the bluegrass festival

my mother
taught me to breathe
in the beauty and peace
of art galleries
where today Andy Warhol's
Muhammad Ali portraits
force air into my lungs
along with the delicious fact
that Eduardo Paolozzi
is Scottish

I walk outside
under cotton-fat clouds
and a windy blue sky
pass two old ladies
laughing on the corner
years and magic
thump in my bones

she
homeless
picks from her full bag
of sweetened popcorn

she
voice like honey
smoothing over
the ache of her words
sits on a stage

in front of
her mottled audience

she
geriatric
earthy
boob job
a rhinestone-studded
pink cowboy hat
and a t-shirt proclaiming
that real objects
are larger than they appear

she
tall
muscles rippling down her arms
braids to her waist
and a squirrely white man
by her side

she
slick
professionally dressed
sagging breasts
stands with a man
whose pants are so stiff
he will be standing
all afternoon

she
maternal
thick
made-up
in her purple stretch
polyester dress
clutching the hand

of the first man I had coffee with
after my husband moved out
      his face shaky with nerves
      under a black cowboy hat
      that same man
      went to war twice
      now he's nervous
      to sing in front
      of a bunch of hippies

me
at peace
alone
in sisterhood
on my center bleacher
watching
listening
thankful
my choices have not made me
the subject of those songs
that fill up
this afternoon sky
with sorrow

EPILOGUE:

person. woman. poem.

Spring, 2021

for Theresa and Rebecka

following years of heartache and tragedy
an injury to my left hand
brings me to physical therapy
twice a week
during the pandemic

this is more touch on my body
than I've known for some time

the lovelies knead
stretch
massage
my crookedness and pain
my heartbreak and broken
we share stories and laugh

something inside me is waking up

are you going on a date?
Rebecka asks when I show up in a dress

you should be going on a date
Theresa says
shows me a picture of F
a friend who is also trying to start over
after devastating loss

she gives me his number
I don't get around to texting F for another week
prolonging possibility

he is cheerful
thoughtful
intelligent

also pleased with himself
and he voted for Trump

twice

and he works in law enforcement

well?
Theresa asks
he is lovely
I tell her
but he's mad conservative

so? at least go for dinner

still
a day of giddy texting
with a handsome stranger
opened something up

I create a profile online

I meet a nurse/musician downtown for donuts
we share dating stories
I mention my collection of poems
why an author writes to a guy holding a fish
written over a decade ago

he laughs
women are holding fish too!
he asks why the poems are still huddled together on my computer
trust me, attack

over donuts and coffee
we talk and talk and talk
many unfinished conversations
mutual enthusiasm and delight

or so it seems

I dream I am on a motorcycle
drive into traffic
and turn sideways
waiting for the crash

I wake up with a scream in my mouth

I had a date I say
as Rebecka folds my stiff fingers forward
I move my other hand
under my leg
so I don't accidentally smack her
and? she asks

it was lovely
and we seemed to click
and then nothing

that's what F says too
Theresa says
lots of ghosting
you should have gone out with F

I delete my profile
submit *why an author writes to a guy holding a fish*
change jobs
visit Houri
and write
another poem

    and another

        and another

the end

ABOUT THE POET

PHOTO:Shelley Welander

LAILA HALABY lives in Tucson, Arizona, where she works as a counselor, creative writing teacher, and museum educator. She is the author of two novels, *Once in a Promised Land* (2007) and *West of the Jordan* (2003). *why an author writes to a guy holding a fish* is Halaby's second collection of poetry. ∎

OTHER BOOKS BY 2LEAF PRESS

2Leaf Press challenges the status quo by publishing alternative fiction, non-fiction, poetry and bilingual works by activists, academics, poets and authors dedicated to diversity and social justice with scholarship that is accessible to the general public. 2Leaf Press produces high quality and beautifully produced hardcover, paperback and ebook formats through our series: *2LP Explorations in Diversity, 2LP University Books, 2LP Classics, 2LP Translations, Nuyorican World Series,* and *2LP Current Affairs, Culture & Politics.* Below is a selection of 2Leaf Press' published titles.

2LP EXPLORATIONS IN DIVERSITY
Substance of Fire: Gender and Race in the College Classroom
by Claire Millikin
Foreword by R. Joseph Rodríguez, Afterword by Richard Delgado
Contributed material by Riley Blanks, Blake Calhoun, Rox Trujillo

Black Lives Have Always Mattered
A Collection of Essays, Poems, and Personal Narratives
Edited by Abiodun Oyewole

The Beiging of America:
Personal Narratives about Being Mixed Race in the 21st Century
Edited by Cathy J. Schlund-Vials, Sean Frederick Forbes, Tara Betts
with an Afterword by Heidi Durrow

What Does it Mean to be White in America?
Breaking the White Code of Silence, A Collection of Personal Narratives
Edited by Gabrielle David and Sean Frederick Forbes
Introduction by Debby Irving and Afterword by Tara Betts

2LP CLASSICS
Adventures in Black and White
Edited and with a critical introduction by Tara Betts
by Philippa Duke Schuyler

Monsters: Mary Shelley's Frankenstein and Mathilda
by Mary Shelley, edited by Claire Millikin Raymond

2LP TRANSLATIONS
Birds on the Kiswar Tree
by Odi Gonzales, Translated by Lynn Levin
Bilingual: English/Spanish

Incessant Beauty, A Bilingual Anthology
by Ana Rossetti, Edited and Translated by Carmela Ferradáns
Bilingual: English/Spanish

NUYORICAN WORLD SERIES
Our Nuyorican Thing, The Birth of a Self-Made Identity
by Samuel Carrion Diaz, with an Introduction by Urayoán Noel
Bilingual: English/Spanish

Hey Yo! Yo Soy!, 50 Years of Nuyorican Street Poetry,
The Collected Works of Jesús Papoleto Meléndez
Bilingual: English/Spanish

LITERARY NONFICTION
No Vacancy; Homeless Women in Paradise
by Michael Reid

The Beauty of Being, A Collection of Fables, Short Stories & Essays
by Abiodun Oyewole

TRAVELOGUE
The Wanderer
by Carole J. Garrison

WHEREABOUTS: Stepping Out of Place,
An Outside in Literary & Travel Magazine Anthology
Edited by Brandi Dawn Henderson

PLAYS
Rivers of Women, The Play
by Shirley Bradley LeFlore, with photographs by Michael J. Bracey

AUTOBIOGRAPHIES/MEMOIRS/BIOGRAPHIES
Trailblazers, Black Women Who Helped Make America Great
American Firsts/American Icons (Volumes 1-3)
by Gabrielle David

Mother of Orphans
The True and Curious Story of Irish Alice, A Colored Man's Widow
by Dedria Humphries Barker

Strength of Soul
by Naomi Raquel Enright

Dream of the Water Children:
Memory and Mourning in the Black Pacific
by Fredrick D. Kakinami Cloyd
Foreword by Velina Hasu Houston, Introduction by Gerald Horne
Edited by Karen Chau

The Fourth Moment: Journeys from the Known to the Unknown, A Memoir
by Carole J. Garrison, Introduction by Sarah Willis

POETRY
PAPOLíTICO, Poems of a Political Persuasion
by Jesús Papoleto Meléndez
with an Introduction by Joel Kovel and DeeDee Halleck

Critics of Mystery Marvel, Collected Poems
by Youssef Alaoui, with an Introduction by Laila Halaby

shrimp
by jason vasser-elong, with an Introduction by Michael Castro
The Revlon Slough, New and Selected Poems
by Ray DiZazzo, with an Introduction by Claire Millikin

A Country Without Borders: Poems and Stories of Kashmir
by Lalita Pandit Hogan, with an Introduction by Frederick Luis Aldama

Branches of the Tree of Life
The Collected Poems of Abiodun Oyewole 1969-2013
by Abiodun Oyewole, edited by Gabrielle David
with an Introduction by Betty J. Dopson

2LEAF PRESS
FLORIDA | NEW YORK
www.2leafpress.org